# Dreams in Motion
# A Collection of Poems and Short Stories

"Poetry is Life…and Life is a Dream in Motion."

## By: Storm

ISBN: Title ID: 3331036
ISBN-13: 978-0615836898

## DEDICATION

To my grandparents Yvonne and Jazz Siler
thank you for always believing in me even
when I didn't believe in myself.

# Contents

The Ugly

# ACKNOWLEDGMENTS

I would like to acknowledge God for all his blessings.
Without him none of this would ever be possible!

# Dreams in Motion

Poetry is an art of expression, but it is more than that.

It is a glimpse into the soul of the story teller and a window into the world of another person.

Poetry is powerful. Words can inspire us, provoke us to rage, bring us close to one another, make us happy, and make us sad.

It takes us from one emotion to the next covering every spectrum of the human existence and experience.

It is an expression of art and emotion through spoken and written words.

It is the stories from the mouths of griots that traveled the middle passage carrying our history in their belly.

It is the song of the field slave that began as a prayer in a whisper of freedom, and ended as a tribute to the past in the mouths of children during black history month.

It is the hook of your favorite song that
started as a line in the mind of an artist
that he could not shake.

It is the flawless movements of a dancer
that started as the awkward pirouettes of a
little girl in her ballet class mirror.

It is the first dance of a bride and groom
that started as a mutual glance of two
strangers across a crowded room.

It is the birth of a child that started as hope
in the hearts of her parents.

It is laughter, heart break, hopes, dreams,
love, hate, defeat, triumph, happiness,
sadness, struggle and faith…It is life.

Poetry is life and life is a dream in motion.

This collection of poems and short stories
covers the gamut of the human
experience…the good…the bad and the
ugly side of life. I write from emotion---I
don't know any other way to do it; so this
collection covers my joys, pains, triumphs

and heartbreaks as well as experiences I have observed from others.

This book will carry you on a journey through every emotion in the spectrum; there are pieces that will make you laugh, cry, get angry, hope, reminisce and think. Some may not agree with what I have written or how I have chosen to write it, but reality and emotions are raw and uncut and so is this collection.

I guarantee that everyone who reads this book will find at least one sentiment expressed in these writings that you can relate to. In essence sometimes in life you have to take the good along with the bad and the ugly.


Can you handle it? If so, turn the page and enter the eye.

嵐 Storm

# The

# Good

This section includes poems that are positive, uplifting and represent the beautiful side of life, love and the human experience.

# The Code of the Black Woman

Your strength within…you cannot hide

It's in your smile…your style…and stride

It's in your eyes…and tears you've cried

It's in your voice…that's filled with pride

In your heart…your dreams abide

Success for you…won't be denied

Failure awaited…those who have tried

To strip you of…your respect…and pride

# Daughter of the Sun

This poem is inspired by one of my favorite poems, "Phenomenal Woman" and dedicated to its author, Maya Angelou, a truly phenomenal writer and individual.

I...AM...BEAUTIFUL!

Why?

Because all black women are, so that includes me.

But, I don't have to tell you that because it is all too easy to see.

From the shape of my lips...to the curve of my hips

I am the very essence of a queen!

From skin dark to fair...permed or natural hair

I am a wonder to be seen!

When I walk, no matter where…everyone
will stop and stare

Amazed at what they saw…they would
stand in total awe.

It's my style, my grace and my soul…a
true beauty to behold!

A beauty that is often imitated…but can
never be duplicated!

Because you see there is only one…true
daughter of the sun.

So if you didn't before…now you see

Black is beautiful and beautiful is me!

# Hostile Take Over

Urban girl in a suburban world

Trying to find your way

Like contraband in a foreign land,

You are feeling a little displaced

And just like rain on the 4th of July,

You are an unwelcome arrival

But just like a well-trained navy seal,

You are a pro at survival

So when "We don't want your kind here"

Are the looks they give to warn

Lace up your "Tims"

Stand your ground

And take the world by storm

# Options

I don't have a choice in succeeding.

I don't have the option to fail.

I hold more than the weight of the world
on my shoulders.

I hold the hopes, dreams and aspirations of
my ancestors.

I breathe because of their sacrifices.

I learn because of their courage.

I walk freely on streets paved by the blood
of my forefathers and the tears of their
mothers.

I climb on the whipped scarred backs of
those who suffered so that I could be
treated as human.

I am pulled through this life by the callous
filled hands of the field slave and the
sharecropper.

I am lifted up on the shoulders of those

that have been beaten down by racism and hate so that I may reach the promise land.

I am the product of more than four hundred years of strength, pride, faith, hope and determination.

I am the prayer on the lips of every African living as Americans that watched their loved ones dragged, beaten and lynched... because "they did not know their place".

So you ask me...why don't I have the option to fail?

It is because my ancestors paid for my right to be treated as human with their lives...that I have any options at all...Any questions?

# Glass Ceilings

Sometimes in life we start off with the best intentions.

We have dreams about how we want our lives to be…

And we are led to believe if we follow certain steps to achieve these dreams…everything will turn out like we plan.

But when we try to follow these steps and it does not work out that way…we are faced with the reality that life isn't always fair.

And that just because you do your best… it doesn't mean you will get the best results.

It is at this point that we feel like we should just give up our dreams…and just be content with surviving.

After being kicked in the teeth so many times… it makes it hard to keep smiling.

After continuously looking at our dreams
through a glass ceiling… and our head
begins to hurt from constantly hitting it on
that glass…we start to accept that we will
never get around it.

And we become content to watch other
people live out our dreams.

This is something that happens way too
often to young Africans living as
Americans.

We are told we have no right to the
American dream, but this is not true.

Our ancestors paid for that right with their
blood, sweat and tears long ago…

And for this reason, we should never
accept someone else dictating to us what
we are destined to be.

We came from a culture of people that has
survived an endured more suffering than
we could imagine, so that we could
achieve our own "American Dream"!

These people have made it to the other

side of that glass despite the odds… and their spirit is in us all.

So when you feel like giving up… and you grow tired of trying to get around that glass…

Close your eyes… Listen carefully… and you can hear the voices of our ancestors saying…"don't give up on your dreams".

And they will give you the strength you need to get through it.


KEEP BREAKING THROUGH THOSE GLASS CEILINGS!

# Diamonds in the Rough

They came from various backgrounds...these black diamonds of Africa and the Caribbean.

Great warriors, kings, doctors & philosophers, were captured and sold as slaves like horses are sold as beast of burden.

They were taken away from their homes, separated from their families and sent to a foreign land as captives.

They were once strong protectors of their families, now they stand helpless as they watch their families destroyed.

They watched their wives be raped and made the object of the slave master's perverted desires.

They watched her give birth to children whose African blood was diluted with the European blood of her rapist.

They watched as their own children were sold off like horses. Once proud warriors were now demeaned and denied the right to be a man; stripped of their pride and dignity.

Once proud names they bore of meaning were replaced with boy and nigger.

Once great philosophers whose thoughts were respected and admired by their people, were now being told that what they think is irrelevant; and that they have no opinion except the one given to them by their master.

Throughout history these diamonds have been beaten in the dirt, broken down and almost crushed; so over the years they have lost their shine.

It was hidden.

Hidden by the mud of prison walls, by the smudges of illiteracy and by the dirty veil of all the years European society spent making the black man feel and act like a non-human, subservient beast of burden….A slave for European society that did not deserve the respect, dignity, or right to be called a man.

So sisters, when you see one of these dirty rocks, don't toss it away....It's fragile, from years of the wear and tear of racism and discrimination.

Pick it up, and gently brush away the years of dirt caused by the black man's struggle to survive in America.

Polish it up with love, encouragement, and understanding.

Lift it up, by helping him regain his dignity, pride and self-respect.

Once this is done, you can see you did not have a worthless rock at all; you had a diamond in the rough.

Then stand back and admire the beauty of the black man.

# **Prelude to a Storm**

PUSH!

Is what I heard the doctor say…as I…went
into labor on my sixteenth birthday.

The pain was so intense it
shook…my…soul…as I…grit my teeth
and…PUSHED… as I was told.

Then…shortly after midnight…the lips
between my hips gave birth to new life.

Though it was never said…it WAS
implied…and understood…that I had just
given sacrifice to my childhood.

The doctor spanked her to initiate the
screams of life…and to signify the end of
the longest night OF MY LIFE!

The doctor placed her in my
arms…smiling saying it's a girl

And immediately…she seemed to be…the
most beautiful girl in the world!

Small and pale with a head full of coal
black hair...I stared at her intently...10
fingers...10 toes...relieved that there all
there!

It was May 3, 1975...clear
morning...bright sky...with a breeze that
was warm

I stared in her eyes...and realized...I had
just given birth to a STORM!

# The Birth of a Storm

You are probably wondering why I choose
to use the name storm.

Well sit back and listen as I spin the tale of
how I came to be born.

Bastard spawn of a wild child and father
without a name, I crossed burning sands
and traveled to lands that could drive any
mind insane.

My complexity causes wonder in those of
curious mind.

They bolster to draw closer in seek of all
they can find.

They long to know the story behind the
eyes with an Asian slant, 'cause my
features are not typical of pure African
descent.

My eyes, my nose, and skin with freckled
hue, call some to pose the question "who
are you?"

My name is storm and since the day I was born my secret has well been kept.

Underestimation of my determination is a quality on which most have slept.

But to their surprise and sometimes demise there is much more than meets their eyes, to the woman they spin their web of lies in hopes to win her soul as their prize.

Before their quest they should have known, better men have tried and their covers were blown.

When you chase a storm in hopes to glance, at the mystery of its beauty you take a chance.

The roll of my thunder makes you lose control... The showers of my rain drops will sooth your soul.

The feel of my warm breeze makes your passion ignite... But deadly is my lightening if I choose to strike.

So beware storm chasers…

Know your soul and your mind… Are
strong enough to with stand the force of
what you'll find.

If I become your next quest…Know these
qualities I will test.

Only those with pure intent and a heart
that is warm… Possess the qualities
needed …To endure this storm

# Perfectly Imperfect

I woke up this morning feeling sexy and free...I was loving everything about me....From the style of my hair even down to my draws... I was loving every part of me ya'll...Even my flaws!

In recent years time has not been kind...By adding a few more inches to my waistline. But it's ok if they say...I'm not runway model material. No, that's not me...And will never be...Unless tomorrow I awake to some small miracle

Or I get nipped and tucked...But then what? We all have imperfections...

And subjecting my life to a surgeon's knife will only make a few corrections

But it won't change the main thing that means more than all else...which is not how the world sees me...But how I see myself.

Yeah there's a little more size on my
thighs than when I was twenty...

But the lessons I learned over these years
I've earned are the true definition of me.

So if you're looking for perfection to form
a connection...Please pardon my
rejection...because you are not for
me...See my soul mate will look for the
true me in my eyes...Not my jean
size...Cause there is more to me than what
you see.

So to all my perfectly imperfect people I
have this to say...Embrace your flaws
ya'll...Its God's signature that you are an
original...And he don't make mistakes.

# While Coltrane Was Playing

Staring at you through eyes unfamiliar, I am seeing you in a different light.

Maybe it's the Coltrane playing...or the words that you're saying...or maybe it's just the Potomac at night.

My mind starts swaying while Coltrane is playing...Touching my spirit with every note. Staring at you I see in your eyes the very essence of my soul.

But how could this be...that you know me...so very well?

We only met twice...and although that was nice...this feeling is crazy as hell.

Though spring is the season to defy all reason and throw caution to the wind. I am not quite sure I have ever felt this before... So I don't know where to begin.

Maybe it's the wine I am sipping that has
me tripping and making the mood feel
right. Or maybe my game started slipping
when we were tongue kissing and
watching the Potomac at night.

I am not sure of our destination or what
our future may hold.

But I know my mind started
swaying…while Coltrane was
playing…and in your eyes I saw my soul.

# More Than a Fairy Tale

Like every little girl I often dreamed of
who my prince charming would be.

He would be handsome and brave and
surpass all odds to sweep me off my feet.

He would be the man of my dreams who
would love to adorn me with silver and
with gold....I would be the envy of all
because I had more happiness than my
heart could ever hold.

Now that I'm grown I realize prince
charming does not exist....He won't ride
to my rescue on a white stead or awaken
me with a kiss.

But when I felt that all was lost and there
was nothing I could do....God sent me a
beautiful gift...and yes that gift was you.

No you did not ride up on a great white
horse like I pictured as a little girl.

But you did show me that there were still
some good men left in the world.

When I need you, with no hesitation you are always there....You place my needs above your own to show how much you care.

In this world which can be so dark, you are the sun that has shone through.

And I hope you know how much I appreciate everything you do.

I pray for you every night that in a world that can be lonely and cold.

God will fill your life with more happiness than your heart has room to hold.

# If

If I was a painter…I would paint a world full of color for my friend and lover…who is one and the same….I would paint a picture of a girl to share his world… and…she would have a face just like mine…and…she would be fine…with…sexy lips, enticing hips and kisses sweet as wine.

If I was a singer…I would sing the sweetest melody… in the perfect key… so that you could see …just how much you mean to me…The strings of your heart I would stroke…with every note…that dripped from my lips causing you to be whipped...and your body to spasm from the mental orgasm my words would create.

Then…I would again pick up my brush…and begin slow…never rush…as I paint a world where there's just us…in love and in lust…gentle kisses and strong thrust. My body shivering from your touch...no doubt we're in love.

But sadly...I can't hold a note or wield a
paint brush to stroke...so I have to use
these words I just wrote to let you
know...my heart sings when you touch
me...symphony when you make love to
me...a world full of color is what you
bring to me...when that sexy smile you
give to me.

Can't begin to say what you mean to me,
so I will simply say loving you is like the
sweetest melody sung in the perfect key or
an artist's masterpiece. No man could
have created thee...so I know your
existence is heavenly.

You are the perfect design...God perfectly
matched your heart to mine...a love so
rare it's one of a kind...so far beyond
words I have to end with this line.

# Chocolate

My momma always told me…"Men are
like a box of chocolates…You never know
what you're gonna get".

From skin that is caramel brown to as deep
and dark as the sweetest chocolate bar…
There is no greater temptation than the
black man!

But as with anything…you can have too
much of a good thing!

My man activates my sweet tooth…and in
feeding my sugar addiction… raises my
blood sugar level to the point I need an
insulin shot…to combat the sugar shock
he sends my body through.

Sweet convulsions of mixed emotions
doing a balancing act between pleasure
and pain.

Withdrawal symptoms come when I miss
him…and slowly drive me insane.

I'm like a fiend…if you know what I
mean, searching for his special mix.

I wait breathless…as I watch him
undress…to give me my chocolate fix.

# A Truly Religious Experience

Conceptualize... you between my thighs planting kisses that make my knees weak.

Imagine...hidden within the lips between my hips... is the treasure you seek.

Reminisce...on your favorite lollipop and keep licking...and licking...'til you've consumed every drop.

Realize...once you taste my sweet center...how many licks did it take to get there...oh boy you won't remember.

As my... body catches the spirit while you speak in tongues causing me to call out the Lord's name...No not in vain... because it is truly a religious experience.

As you...wade in the water of the storm you just created...

And you...swing low your sweet chariot that is...cumin forth to carry me home...

Brace your hips 'cause I'm cumin up the
rough side of the mountain...But I won't
be cumin alone.

I'm going to let my little light shine...as
we climb those stairways to heaven...

Showing amazing grace as I increase the
pace of how my hips are moving

Recognize... you have found a place
where you can lay your burdens down...

Cause aint nothing in the world... sweeter
than how my orgasms sound...

As our tension mounts we've lost count of
the number of orgasms between us...

But I'll scream hallelujah as I'm cumin
onto you ...because it is truly a religious
experience.

# Breathe

Breathe…Is what my mind told my lungs to do when the first sight of you took my breath away.

It is what I did when I inhaled the scent of your essence left by your presence in my bed this morning.

It's the sweet exhale that signals the cessation of our lovemaking session that ended at sunrise.

It's the rhythmic melody our bodies sing in unison as our souls intertwine to become one.

It's what my daddy said…as he led me down the aisle to become your wife.

It's what you whispered in my ear as you held my hand…and delivered your seed into the existence of life.

It's what I do deeply… when thoughts of you pervade my subconscious and my love for you shows on my face.

It's what I held patiently for the one God made just for me…

And then that package from heaven that is you was sent…with a message from God written on your lips…delivered in our first kiss that said…

Just breathe.

# Easy As a Sunday Morning

On a Sunday morning that started like any other…My routine was interrupted when I saw this SEXY brother! This man had me hypnotized I don't even remember blinking…Just asking God's forgiveness for the thoughts that I was thinking.

Yeah I know that church was not the place for thoughts of romance…But there was no well in hell I was going to pass up this chance. So I made my way down to the place where he stood…While thinking to myself "damn this man looks good!"

I tried not to stare and kept my composure…I couldn't risk my intentions receiving exposure. The usher began seating us on one row at a time…

And I couldn't help but pray that his row would be mine.

I guess God was listening and answered

my prayers…Because when I looked up he was standing right there. I tried to play it cool like his presence didn't matter…Periodically engaging him in idle chit chatter.

My eyes were on the pulpit but my mind wondered through…The thoughts of who he would be going home to. The pastor's lips were moving but I didn't hear a thing…I was too busy checking his hand for a ring.

But I did tune in for some things he would say…Like his "hug your neighbor" line came in handy that day. It presented an opportunity to start a conversation…One that I welcomed with no hesitation.

We laughed and chatted until the end of the service…But the thought of never seeing him was making me nervous. I tried to relax and appear real casual…But I was happy to discover the interest was mutual.

We shared a connection that surged with power…And continued to increase with each passing hour. From that day forward we became inseparable...And our sexual energy became immeasurable.

It was like a dream with the perfect woman and man...But when the dream was over reality set in. His signs of affection were replaced with irritation...

And I began to wonder if it was just my imagination.

Did we share a connection or was it just a lie...That I told myself when I looked into his eyes? If we were connected I should know what to say...

To decrease his pain I see growing each day.

When I watch him sleep with no sign of peace...I just want to hold him until his worries decrease. He told me his rough season in life he doesn't expect me to...Understand, stand by his side, or help to see him through.

Now usually he is perceptive, but in this case he was wrong. Friends are there through every season no matter how rough or long. When the winds of life's storms attempt to sweep him away…I will be his anchor to keep him grounded and safe.

In all he may face whether he loses or wins…As easy as that Sunday morning, I'll stand right beside him.

# The
# Bad

This section contains poems and short stories that explore those everyday difficulties that happen in various aspects of love, faith and life. The language and content of some of these works may not be suitable for some readers so proceed with caution.

# My Apology

I feel I owe you an apology…for not
giving you a chance to love the real me.

When I look in your eyes, it's not me that
I see…it's more like a shell of who I
thought you wanted me to be.

This person I don't know…or even
recognize… she is just a symbol of all I've
sacrificed.

You never asked me to be this person that
I see…no her existence was cultivated by
me.

Though the ingredients I used were
inspired by you…or by being who I
thought you wanted me to.

I am not sure where I lost myself and
began this charade...not sure of the name
for the character I played.

I think a chameleon would best describe
it…because it would change to whatever I
thought would fit.

Reserved, supportive, passive and laid
back…I let YOUR mood determine how I
would act.

I spent most of our time together tailoring
what you would see…so much so I forgot
how to be me…at least with you.

In my farce I think I was unfair…you
never got to see the real woman standing
there.

I apologize that I let myself forget…and
did not remain the confident, funny, sexy,
flirtatious, vibrant woman you met.

I cheated you out of the opportunity…to
get to know the REAL me.

I hid a lot of who I am…to perfect and
perpetuate this scam.

But in the end…I still lost…because the
woman I am was not the woman you
saw…at least in the end.

All in all I am glad that we met, but in the
future I will remember not to forget…to
be me.

No matter what the circumstance...I will give the next man in my life the chance...to love me...for who I am not who I think he wants me to be.

I will learn from our relationship and acknowledge my part. I won't hide my feelings or guard my heart.

I won't say it is ok when my feelings get hurt. I won't ever forget to value my worth.

I won't make the next man pay for another's mistake. I will remember that love is not only GIVE but also take.

I will always be grateful for my time with you and for every experience we have gone through.

I can truly say you have impacted my life...and now I am ready to be some lucky man's wife...To love that man with my whole heart and let him love the real me...from the very start.

# Same Old Song

Ladies you ever get tired of hearing the
same ole shit...Tired ass lines from men
that just want to hit. Bragging and
boasting about the things that they have
done...And with a sincere face tell you
they think you're the one.

But slowly and surely as time goes
on...You see it's just a different sorry
brotha singing the same old song. I
wonder when their born and begin to
grow...At what point in time are they
taught to be hoes?

Is it done through peer pressure in order to
be cool? Or is this a foundation course
they learn in school? Reading, writing and
arithmetic...Cheating, lying and being a
bitch...

See for some they seem to go hand in
hand...With what some boys think it
means to be a man. In all fairness I can't
say this applies to all...But it damn sure
applies to most of y'all!

At least the ones that I have come across…Who think that being the man means being your boss! But sad to say I been raised once and my daddy you are not! You can't even be a parent to ones you got!

Yeah you give them money for child support…But are you being responsible for what they are taught? Lead by example that's the golden rule…Because they are watching everything you do.

So when you treat their mothers like trash and your girlfriends too…They think that is what a man is supposed to do. To lie and cheat and hurt those who love them…To disrespect women and place everyone above them.

To have love in their heart, but with no one to share…To reach out to find that there is no one there…To realize they have lost the experience of having pure joy…Because every woman that loved them they would only destroy.

What a legacy you have passed on…To
grow cold and distant and end up
alone…Being just another brotha…
Singing YOUR sad ass song!

# Unbreakable

Tossing and turning in search of sleep…
The only state where my mind finds peace

See it's my respite from the pain…That
threatens to drive me insane

Not too fond of being awake…For this is
when my heart seems to break

Tired of being the one who is
strong…Tired of being the one everyone
depends on …

Understanding and there whenever you
need…But, when is someone going to be
there for me?

Tired of meeting "good men" "too late"…
And having to pay for some other
woman's mistakes

Tired of hearing "I am just not ready to
move on"…But they still expect me to be
there for them to lean on

Tired of looking at other people's lives...
and wondering "what happened to mine?"

Tired of trying to do the right thing
...when pain and disappointment is all it
seems to bring

Do you think I'm made of Teflon? And
that my heart can take all the pain you pile
on?

Suicide will never be an option for
me...So what choice do I have but to
continue to be?

Continue to hurt and continue to
cry...Sometimes the ache is how I know I
am alive.

To look at me you would never
know...The depth of the pain I refuse to
show.

You see my smile...you hear my
laugh...But you know nothing about the
truth that they mask...

Took years to rebuild my trust in
you...And you proved that was my

mistake too.

Labeled me as the strong one...The one to call when you need something done

Able to handle anything you do...My purpose for existence is to save you

What will happen on the day...That I am the one who needs to be saved?

Will someone risk their heart to save me... Or let me drown?

Will someone reach for me...Or just let me down?

What will happen I want to know...When the damage I suffered starts to show?

Someone please tell me just what will it take...To show the world that I too can break?

# Love on Lock

My heart is in a box locked away, safe
from the danger called "LOVE".

Love brings with it pain, hurt, loss of
control...Feeling like someone else is the
keeper of your soul.

But I have found the solution...And
gained resolution for the issue at hand.

Like trying to grasp and hold onto
sand...Love slips through your fingers and
disappears...Leaving behind the feeling of
fear...Loneliness...and pain.

Vowing that you will never again give
yourself to another..."Not one more lover
will I let into my bed, my head, or my
heart!

Nah, I will nix that from the start".

So I purchased myself a solid lock to
secure my heart inside that box.

No one can break it and get to me, unless
you are the one with the master key.

That one will be kind...loving...and true.
Could that someone be you?

# Unnecessary Drama

In my distress I wrote Caress to check the unbelievable. Could it be the soap I used that made me appear invisible? See that's the only explanation I could find for my implied transparency. And that's the only logical excuse to behave like you couldn't see me.

You looked right through me everyday like a window without a pane...fostering insecurities to slowly drive me insane. You chipped away at my spirit with every lie you told...clouding my mind with confusion like a window frosted by the cold.

I love you was the biggest lie to me you ever said. How the hell can you love me in someone else's bed? Each betrayal was like a rock hitting against a glass...And every day I wondered if I'd ever forget your ass.

Although you tried to break me, and the shit you did was wrong. You'll find that I'm still standing...you'll find that I'm still strong. The pain I feel will disappear and all my tears will dry. I finally have the strength I need to say my last goodbye.

Right now you may be laughing and feeling like you've won. But it'll come back to haunt you before it's said and done. You may not see it now, but very soon you will. And you will have to pay for all the pain you made me feel.

I won't want your apology, or to hear about your regrets. One day I will forgive you, but I will never forget. All is fair in love and war, but you're not worth the fight. So I don't need your sorry ass, 'cause I will be all right.

# Why?

Why do we hold on to people who don't want to be held?

Why do we cling to feelings that are no longer felt?

Why do we make excuses for people who do us wrong?

Why do we deny what we've known all along?

Why do we seek advice but refuse to take it?

Why do we know it's over but continue to fake it?

Why do we ignore what is right in front of us?

Why do we stay with those we can't trust?

Why do we embrace those that make us cry?

Why do we listen to lie after lie?

Why do we put up with the same old bullshit?

Why do we expect this time it will be different?

Why do we accept abuse and disrespect?

Why do we feel we should take what we can get?

Why do we take advice from those in the same situation?

Why do we believe their advice with no hesitation?

Why do we place another's welfare above ourselves?

Why do we continue to reside in hell?

Why do we know to stay would be insane?

Why do we know this, but yet we remain?

Why do we value their occasional
affection more than we do our health?

Why do we expect to be loved when we
do not love ourselves?

# Enough Is Enough

You know it's amazing what we as
women become accustomed to.

We get so use to being mistreated; we
praise things you're supposed to do.

Like take care of your kids, give us
respect, and pay your share of the bills.

We form our lives around YOUR needs
and ignore the way WE feel.

No, I don't want to stay at home and place
you in charge of my fate…

But I do expect you to work, be a man and
pull your own weight.

See I am your woman, your friend and
your African-American Queen.

Not your momma, your ho, or your maid
that cooks and cleans.

So respect me and cherish me, for I am
your greatest wealth…

And I won't accept anything less because I love and respect myself.

So I am telling you this in hopes that it is something you can feel...

Because if you can't be the King for this Queen, I'll find someone who will!

# You've Changed

You've changed…he said to me…looking…quite curiously…as if trying detect…this new defect…he has found in my persona.

You've changed…no it's not how you wear your hair or the style of clothes you wear….but there is something definitely amiss.

You've changed…you don't respond the same when I touch you…or go to kiss or hug you…though the change is subtle…it has me befuddled…and I can't quite put my finger on it…but I know I don't like it.

You've changed…and I don't know why…but I feel you owe me an explanation…for your hesitation when I call your name.

You've changed and I am confused…because I…have remained the same.

So I said...I've changed...oh yes this is
true...see I don't tolerate the same things
that I use to...like
disrespect...selfishness...and utter
disregard.

Try to focus on the words I am
saying...though I know...for you this is
hard.

See for you to focus on my words...you
would have to pay attention...which is
something you failed to do...among other
things I'll mention.

Like put me first...commit to me...and
show me that you care...not just call my
name in the heat of passion...then behave
like I'm not there.

Or make false promises...that to me you'll
never keep...like making sure in our
bed...is the only place you'll sleep.

I've changed...I love myself more than I
love your abuse...no you have never put
your hands on me...but emotionally...I
am black and blue.

See you have beat me down with infidelity…lies…and neglect…there is only so much one person can take…so what did you expect?

I found someone who's my best friend…he attentive…passionate and loving…If you weren't always out with your boys...you might have seen this coming.

Oh don't try look heartbroken…for that you don't have the knack…so save all your tears and fake promises...because they will not win me back.

Learn from this…so next time you meet a queen you'll know just how to treat her…take care of her heart…put her first…and show her that you need her.

Take head to this message…it can change your whole world…cause while you were out with your boys…someone else took your girl.

# The Mass Production of Spirituality

The mass production of spirituality ... the mass production of spirituality

Step right up ...save your soul... tell the devil he has lost control

We are a massive church with a massive heart...who believe in giving...your tithes are a good start

Yes there a good start saints but that is only one...don't forget the love offering...pastor appreciation...pastor anniversary...pastor needs a new Benz and of course...the building fund!

The revolution will not be televised...but my sermon will... in the plasma screened media room...you'll help to build

We have every accommodation for a church of the new millennium...sky lights...auditorium seating...and of course...an ATM!

See we don't want you to have an excuse
not to pay your dues…no that's not
enough money sistah…no reach again
brotha…I'm sure there's more you can do!

See God gave me a vision that said some
of you are holding out…but believe me
it's your salvation I am really worried
about!

If you don't give all you can…how can I
pay for my latest vacation…umm…I
meant… how can you achieve your
salvation?

Besides your tithes are the least you can
do…you shouldn't mind…a little extra on
side… to pay for the show I give you!

I'm educated…well spoken…and know
just what to say…You get the chance to
see my song and dance at three shows…I
mean…services… every Sunday!

Because remember like 7-11 we are
always open to serve you…just don't ask
for spiritual counseling…because that…I
don't do!

Unless you are a VIP...AKA...very
wealthy...then...I am available...see
because to me...more money... makes
your soul more savable!

I know that some may say...it doesn't cost
anything to pray...but those prayers were
not mine...its different see...when prayer
comes through me...because only I...
have God's direct line!

From my point of view...I'd change a
word or two...from some motivational
sayings...Just one or two... would make
them true...about the way that I view
praying!

No sistah you can't get me...for family
counseling when your marriage faces bad
weather... unless you can give a little
more on Sunday morning cause...the
family that PAYS together...STAYS
together!

Don't you see...salvation isn't free...you
have to PAY to PRAY!

I am in much too big a hurry…to
schmooze with Halle Berry …to listen to
what YOU have to say!

Well you know how the saying goes…I've
got places to go…and rich people to see

But let me leave you with this reality…the
mass production of spirituality…is only a
fallacy!

# Mask

I am wearing a mask right now…in fact I have a few

I put them on so that you will see…only what I want you to

I have one bearing a fictitious smile…to hide my very real tears

I have one with a courageous glare…to conceal my terrifying fears

I have one expressing sheer joy…to hide my heart wrenching pain

I have one on most every day…it's all a part of the game

# Have You Seen Me?

Someone once told me that one-day I
would find peace of mind, but they
neglected to tell me where to look.

So I search… speeding down life's
highway with no visible map, clear
directions, or set destination.

My mind is full of random thoughts,
visions of my past, frustration of my
present, uncertainty of my future.

My soul is restless…my mind longing for
peace.

Searching for happiness…a clue to where
my peace of mind lay…but all I find is
confusion.

Struggling to survive in a world that can
be so cold…

Not knowing exactly where I fit…but
knowing I am a part of the puzzle.

Unsure of my purpose…but knowing I have one.

No clear direction… but traveling just the same.

Longing for the other half of myself…but not sure where to look…

Loving behind a shield…but still being hurt

Wanting to trust…but not sure whom I can.

Walking through a haze of emotions…searching for myself

Have you seen me?

# The "Me" I am Supposed to Be

Yo it's been cool, but I think we should part ways…See you're reminiscent of my wilder days

Back when I was younger and running the streets…and the only one I cared about pleasing was me.

See I am older now and a lot more wise…so I know dealing with you will be my demise.

See all you wanna do is party and have fun…but when it comes to priorities…you have none!

Running with you…I felt like I was grown…and I forgot about everything I learned at home!

What home training? …you must be insane when…you ask me if this is how I was raised! I'm doing me…so you see…I don't need your praise.

'Cause life's a game and…things aren't
the same when…you don't play your part.

I didn't realize behind that disguise…I
became someone that had no heart.

I didn't give a (what)…so it was just your
bad luck… if you happen to run into me.

Cause I would take you for a ride…then
strip you of your pride…oh there was
much more to me than what you see.

I thought my vision was clearer…and my
game was thorough as can be…until I
looked in the mirror and I didn't like who
stared back at me.

See it was you I saw…with no traces of
the old me…I realized…I missed who I
use to be.

So this is goodbye…that's it…we're
through…leaving you behind is what I got
to do.

Party's over…time to leave…my time
with you…I will not grieve.

Truthfully…I'm glad we are
done…because life with you really wasn't
that fun…I lost a lot more than I
gained…so to keep you around would be
insane!

I have to go now…I have someone to
see…it's been too long since she's seen
me.

Yeah she's the one I use to be…back in
the day when I liked being me.

Back before I met you…now she's the one
I'm going back to.

So tomorrow when I look in the mirror
again…I will say hello to my old friend.

I will tell her I am sorry for leaving…and
ask her to forgive me…then I will
embrace her…the me…I am supposed to
be!

# The

# Ugly

These poems and short stories are not for the easily offended or those with virgin ears. It is the representation of the ugly reality of the world we live in…uncut and uncensored. I know some may feel the content is over the top, but just like the age old question "if a tree falls in the forest and no one is around to hear it, does it make a sound?" If the reality of the world is ignored does it make it any less ugly?

# The Game of Street Life

Life is a crazy game, or so the saying goes

Full of pimps, players, tricks, and hoes

I 'm not just talking about the ones in the
street

That will sell their body to any trick for a
treat

No you can find them in any place

Living their lives for the paper chase

Whether chasing money, power, or ….

Either they're tricking, or they're getting
tricked

Pimping or getting pimped, playing or
getting played

Either they're the ones paying or they're
the ones getting paid

However they fit, whatever they're part

Whatever the end, however they start

Everyone has a story to tell

They know their role, and they play it well

But the path of the streets can be a curse

That leads to jail, addiction, and even a hearse

For like a game, life too will end

But in the game of the streets, no one really wins

# Wanted: Someone to Love (by any means necessary)

Every face is different…no name is the same…Every outcome is similar…but who is the blame?

The woman who keeps searching…or the men that she finds…Will any man do? Or is love really blind?

Alcoholics, drug addicts, pushers, and pimps…Is she trying to be saved? Or is she trying to save them?

Whatever her plan or whatever their game…Abused, misused, it all ends the same.

Bloody and bruised, or tears on her pillow…Drinking, smoking and sitting by her window.

With songs in the background telling stories of hearts broken…Mouth trembling, eyes swollen, but no words spoken

But when her tears dry, with fresh make up on her face…Her search begins for another to take his place.

Such a vicious cycle of pleasure and pain…and what an empty existence for this player of the game.

# Jaded

We are so different you and I. We see the world through separate eyes.

Yours are rose colored and good is never faded. Mine see the evil of a world that is jaded.

**You see...** a man in the snow that is down on his luck, trying to hustle to make a quick buck. You imagine life dealt him a bad hand, and that all in all he is really a good man.

The money you give him will feed his family. You never considered his state of insanity. To you he's the beggar and you're the Good Samaritan, trying to become a good humanitarian.

His wife appears loyal to stand by her man, for better or worse in this circumstance. You romanticize their plight like Romeo and Juliet. They are an example of how strong love can get.

**I see…**a junkie who makes his home in the snow, 'cause he traded his rent for another hit of blow. Would sell his soul for that candy for his nose, traded his life with his wife a long time ago

When money got tight turned her into his hoe…sent her feet to the street to walk the stroll. As his need for a fix started to grow, he was a slave and his master was blow.

See that drug cocaine had his brain, systematically driving his ass insane.

To help her deal with johns he turned his wife on, not enough she's his hoe now she's hooked on blow.

Can't feed TWO habits on her back, so they downsized…from blow to crack. Now crack is their only reason to live…For their next hit tried to sell their kids.

Their parental rights came to a stop, 'cause their potential buyer was an undercover cop. Now they're sitting in county doing a bid… blaming each other 'cause the state got their kids.

Their only concern for getting them back
is to find another buyer to trade them for
crack. When you see them you want to
save their soul, but all I see is two junkies
in the snow.

In my view good is faded, so like the
world...I guess I'm JADED.

# Good Intentions

People always want to smother you with those "positive thoughts" everyone says when something goes wrong in other people's lives.

You know what I am saying, things like "That's life", "Life goes on" and my all time favorite, "It happens to the best of us"! Well here's my thought for the day, "Life's A Bitch, Then You Die"!

Call me cynical if you want, but no one really believes that shit. What they really want to say is, "Damn! I'm Glad That Is Not Me!"

I Know, I know, you have to think positive right, well where I'm from positive thoughts don't pay the rent. Hell you can't even get a penny for your thoughts these days.

Yeah, people will kill you with kindness and good intentions, (Shit the road to hell was paved with good intentions). But don't ask them for something you could use, like a loan, then all of a sudden they are not so "Positive" your unemployed ass will get another job to pay them their money back.

Talk is cheap, that is why people are always giving you advice; because in this world honey, that is the only thing that is free!

# Battered Wife Vows

He whispered he loved you with every
thrust

With every blow from his fists he broke
your trust

With those same hands he wiped your
tears

And at some point love was confused with
fear

Kept your vow to love honor and obey

Convinced yourself he would change if
you stay

Lived for him with your every breath

Until the day he loved you to death

Darkness covered you like a flood

As your body lay limp and covered in
blood

No breath in your body...no beat in your

heart

You kept your vows until death you did
part

# The Black Man's Road to Salvation

What I am is what you made me. Cold, mistrustful, only looking out for self

How? If you don't know than you are the one that is delusional. Conjuring up these ideas that we were saved and improved by you, when you came to rescue us "savages" from our heathenish and barbaric ways.

You tried to transform us into these good little trained monkeys, YOU called Christians. You forced us to leave behind our culture, history, and freedom…Making us into slaves…Raping our black women, killing our black men…Whipping and stripping us of our dignity.

Hiding behind bed sheets as you burned our houses and churches, lynched our men and women, and tormented our children. And for what, because we wanted to think

for ourselves, because our skin was
beautiful shades of brown, while yours
was devoid of color?

Where are our forty acres and a mule?
Where is our retribution? Excuse me if I
don't show extreme gratitude, for your
heathenish and barbaric ways of bringing
us to salvation!

## Could It Be?

Could it be, me living in a world that's
stress free? But for me that's not easy to
see, everyone trying to put chains on me,
trying to silence my creativity.

Always talking equality, but don't nobody
give a damn about me.

I'm just another number another welfare
mother one kid on my hip two more beside
me, three more in my future got one in my
belly.

Living out my ghetto dreams while trying
to run another welfare scheme.

Nah ain't no peace for me...ain't no
equality, not as long as all you see...is just
another black monkey...swinging from a
tree.

Yes massa...no massa...those days behind
me...ain't nobody selling me into slavery.
Cook your own food and wash your own
laundry...'cause your ass will starve if you
waiting on me... To do that bull

shit....that master slave shit... I don't play that... can't get wit it!

I the got will...I'll make a way...keep on striving for a better day. Keeping my head up 'cause this shit will pass...and when it does... Well y'all can all kiss what I twist...I don't mean my wrist...can you feel this?

Damn this shit is getting deep....I pray the lord my soul to keep...through this madness...life's insanity. While I struggle to keep my humanity...in a world that can't even see me...But want to be me...and at the same time wants to see me swinging from a tree.

Or laid in bed with master...my life pure disaster...my whole existence to be the slave master's ho. Hell no! Can't be me...it's in my nature to be free... ain't nobody putting chains on me...ain't nobody silencing my creativity.

Damn you and your equality...cause no matter what...I going to be me

Too strong for you to beat...and too black

for you not to see

Can you feel me?

# Short Stories

This section contains short stories that entertain, amuse and teach life lessons. The content and language may vary in this section.

# Old Soul in a New Time

As I ride over dusty country roads lined with trees bearing leaves kissed by autumn; I stare out the window and daydream. The sun shines through the leaves of the trees as it sets on another day and paints the world a haze of color as soft as the glow of a fireplace in winter. I become transformed like I used to play here. Listening to stories of a time when life was simple, my heart feels warm and my soul feels at peace.

My mind starts to wander off, and my imagination sparks visions of myself playing hide and seek amongst those trees with siblings that don't exist. Feeling like a child in the wrong age, I look into the soul of a time long passed. I feel like I've been here before; remembering memories that could not possibly be mine. Maybe it was in a dream I once had. Faces floating in my mind of people I have never met; yet they seem so familiar.

Blues songs fill my head and I imagine a shabby juke joint set off of an old country road, like the one I am traveling. It is filled with awed faces sitting motionless like an imaginary force transfixes them. Their attention is focused on the small stage, where a tall voluptuous woman with caramel colored skin and a voice strong as iron, yet smooth as satin, sways her hips while belting out a melancholy, melody that fills the air like smoke.

She is sharing her pain with world, and with every word she sings, you get a glimpse into her soul. Each note exposes a different chapter of joy, happiness, pleasure, pain and tragedy. I am staring at her now, with the same awed expression as those who now sit under her spell. I stare at her and wonder. Who is she really?

Is she just a brown skin beauty with a hypnotic voice and haunting brown eyes or is she the voice of a nation? Is she the answer to some parents' prayer or the cause of their torment? Is she the fleeting object of most men's desires or the woman of one man's dream? Is she merely a symbol of strength and courage in a time when those characteristics were considered more of a liability than an attribute? No, she is more than that.

I made my way down to the front of the stage to get a closer look. I felt that I had to see her face more clearly to understand who she really was. As I approached, her face came in to focus and I was astonished at my discovery. She was not merely one of those things; she was all of those things. She was my mother, my grandmother, my aunt, my sister, my friend...she was me. But how could this be? These are visions that could not possibly be mine, unless I am an old soul in a new time.

# Pleasure Trip

"Good Morning and thank you for riding Metro" the annoying metro operator pipes in, as you sit there looking around the crowed train; wishing your car was not in the shop. Then all of a sudden, you see this ebony prince with a body like a Mandingo warrior, a smile bright as the sun and eyes so penetrating you become hypnotized! He looks your way, eyes lock and imaginations start thinking of erotic fantasies unexplored. He licks his lips… and suddenly your mind flips to thoughts of those lips pressed against your own, exploring every inch of your body like a detective.

In an instant, everyone and everything around you disappears and your mind sets a scene that is more romantic than your actual surroundings. Idle chit chatter of fellow passengers is replaced by India Arie's song "Brown Skin". The florescent lighting of the train's car is replaced by the soft glow of candlelight. The ugly hard orange seats are now a beautiful soft king sized bed complete with luxurious satin sheets covered in rose petals. Not to mention, plenty of room to try those Kama Sutra moves in that "Joy of Sex" book you received as a Christmas present (and hint that you are long overdue), from your "not so subtle" younger sister.

Slowly, you undress your new found ebony prince and discover what lies under those jeans and timberlands. Your heart is pounding in your chest and your body starts shaking with the anticipation of some serious lovemaking. Standing there in the shadows of the candlelight, your lips find each other and your body is eager to practice making all those grandbabies your mother keeps complaining that she doesn't have.

He picks you up and lays you across the bed. Your bodies intertwine light and dark skin…and your temperature rises until both of your bodies simultaneously explode in ecstasy… bathed in sweat and sweet exhaustion! Just as he is about to tell you that you are the woman that he has waited his entire life for, (*bell sounds, ding dong*) "This is the L'Efant Plaza metro station, door opening on the right"; the annoying metro train operator sends your ass crashing back to reality! As you watch your daydream lover exit the car, you think "Damn! Note to self, buy a flash pass!"

# A Single Red Rose in Her High School Locker

Someone once wrote that everything he needed to know about life he learned in kindergarten. Well everything Jasmine Alexander "Jazz" needed to know about true love she learned in high school. Growing up in Jordan Springs, a small town in North Carolina, you become very familiar with the people around you and they become very familiar with you (mostly because they are always in your business).

You usually go through your school years and growing pains with the same faces you started out with. Some you get to know well and others you just know. This cozy, sometimes claustrophobic, atmosphere could make for archenemies or best friends. In Jazz's case, she met someone who became both.

Jazz met her archenemy/best friend in kindergarten, and he was the person who taught her the meaning of the word hate. Although they became archenemies first and remained as such for a long time, their friendship grew to surpass the term best friends and became first love.

Keeping in mind that Jazz lived in a small town, the selection of boys in her age group that she thought were cute or even interesting was very limited. However, there appeared to be a never ending supply of irritating and obnoxious boys. A fact that made Jazz long for the day she could escape this boring little berg and move on to a place that was filled with fun things to do and interesting people to meet. This particular boy Terrence James "TJ" had all of the bases covered.

TJ was the source of Jazz's torment throughout her school years and she truly felt his purpose for getting up every morning was to make her life hell! Fortunately for her, he was an army brat so he moved around a lot. He would spend one year in their town and the next somewhere else in the world. Jazz lived for the off years when he was anywhere she did not have to see his smug, obnoxious and annoyingly cute face.

Jazz and TJ's "love to hate you" relationship started to shift around the 8th grade. See this is the time when the bodies and hormones of little boys and little girls began to develop at the speed of light; and games like hide and go seek turn into hide and go get (a feel).

Jazz's lifelong archenemy had just come back to their school and she was perfectly content to resume their usual mutual hatred for one another, but this time things were a little different.

All of a sudden, TJ's smug cute face seemed more cute than smug and his usual obnoxious comments bordered more on the side of flirtatious than obnoxious. They even started to have conversations that did not end in heated arguments.

"Could this be the beginning of a truce?" Jazz thought to herself. Before the answer to that question could be revealed he moved away again, but this time…she wasn't as happy to see him go.

The summer before their junior year of high school, gave way to the biggest shift in their roles as archenemies. It was an ordinary summer day in North Carolina, hot and sticky, and Jazz stopped at a convenience store to get something to drink. She had just left volleyball try-outs looking very athletic, but having no actual athletic ability whatsoever!

Jazz was dressed in a pink and white t-shirt and matching running shorts, both of which clung to her now sweaty, but well-developed body. The heat and her state of exhaustion focused Jazz's attention on a cold bottle of water and a very long shower!  She almost didn't notice her archenemy sitting in the car with his best friend Quentin when she exited the store. When she did notice she purposely ignored him.

"Hey what's up girl, you been working out?" Quentin called out as she approached the car. "What's up Q? Nah just came from Volleyball try-outs" Jazz responded coolly trying not to look at TJ.

"Word, so how did it go? You make the team?" Quentin quizzed. "Let's just say that if I had any doubts before, today confirmed that I am not the jock type" Jazz laughed. Jokingly Quentin replied "Well I guess I don't have to ask you when your first game is then huh?"

The two shared a laugh and then to Jazz's surprise, TJ slyly interjected "Well even if you weren't the most athletic on the court, you damn sure had to be the sexiest!" The comment caught her off guard and Jazz stood dumbstruck like a deer in headlights.

It had been two years since Jazz and TJ had last seen each other and to her knowledge he still hated her and vice-versa. "Maybe he is suffering from heatstroke and he forgot that we are sworn enemies. I mean that possible truce in the

8th grade did not mean anything right? "
Jazz thought while trying to figure out
Terrence's angle and how he became so
damn fine over one summer.

"Are you speechless or you just can't
speak to me? The Jasmine Alexander I use
to know was never at a loss for words?"
TJ joked in that familiar voice. That voice
use to be a lot higher and belong to the
obnoxious little boy Terrence, whose
smug face and demonic smile elicited a
nauseating feeling in the pit of her
stomach. Now it was deeper and belonged
to the well-developed young man known
as "TJ", whose gorgeous face and sexy
smile were eliciting another uncomfortable
feeling...but it wasn't nausea!

Not quite sure if this new feeling
showed on her face, Jazz faked her best
nonchalant hello, told Quentin she would
catch him later then immediately left. But
for the first time, she hoped she would see
Terrence again. She did not know exactly
what their new relationship would be now
that he was back, but one thing she did
know it wasn't going to be the same!

Jazz's wish to see TJ again became reality when she went out that night. Jordan Springs or "The Springs" as the locals called it was never known for being a place with a lot of activities for young people to do, so most teenagers made their own fun.

This fun consisted mostly of going to a nearby city to hang out, going to house parties and turning the parking lots of various businesses into an impromptu party. It was at one of these impromptu parties that Jazz realized that not only was TJ no longer her enemy, but their relationship was about to take a 180 degree turn.

Jazz was sitting on her car arguing with Trent, a guy she made the mistake of going on one date with, but had spent most of the night trying to end a relationship that existed only in his mind. Fortunately for Jazz Trent's attention was pulled away when an argument he started earlier with a guy from Westwood, their high school rivals, erupted into a fight.

While Jazz watched the immature exhibition of male stupidity that familiar voice once again captured her interest. "See that wouldn't have happened if you were my girl". Jazz turned around to see the same sexy smile and gorgeous face she had seen earlier that day. "Was she hearing things? Did that corny, but unmistakably flirtatious, statement just come from the person she swore to hate until the day she died? Yep"!

For the majority of the night, TJ had been enjoying the shameless advances of various teenage girls competing in a "who can be the biggest ho competition" where he was the prize. So Jazz didn't even notice that while she was arguing with her insane stalker, TJ was standing behind her watching.

Jazz didn't remember the exact contents of the conversation, but it ended with her and TJ exchanging phone numbers and TJ telling her that they should be together. Jazz never thought it would go anywhere because at the time TJ still lived more than 2 hours away with his mother. She didn't even expect to hear from him again, but she did.

About a week or so later Jazz was standing on a chair changing the light bulb in her room when the phone rang. She almost fell off the chair when she heard TJ's sexy voice say "Hey, what's up?" With a huge smile growing on her face Jazz thought to herself "He actually called!"

The conversation was a continuation of TJ listing reasons why he and Jazz should be together that ended with her saying that he lived too far away. The following week, TJ called to inform her that he moved with his father in Westwood and would now only be 20 minutes away.

"I told you we should be together, its fate" TJ said in his best attempt at being seductive. Jokingly, Jazz quipped "And I told you that if we were not at the same school you were still too far". They chatted for a little longer then said goodbye, but thoughts of exploring this new but strange feeling developing between them, was on both of their minds that night.

TJ and his father did not have the best relationship and he decided he would rather live with his grandmother in Jordan Springs. Jazz's next phone call from TJ was to ask her to meet him at school on Monday to show him around.

That Monday they met in the parking lot and Jazz agreed to share her locker with him. She showed him around, gave him the combination to "their" locker and told him that she would see him later.

At break she went to the locker to get her books for the next class. When she opened the locker Jazz smiled so hard she thought her face would crack. TJ had placed a rose with a little note for her in the locker that simply said "I care about you". This was the beginning of what proved to be one of the most beautiful relationships of Jazz's life.

As with any relationship Jazz and TJ had their share of good times and bad, but the underlying love for each other was always strong. There was never a time that she needed him that he was not there and there was never a time that he needed her that she would not stand by his side.

TJ was her most honest critic, biggest cheerleader, partner in crime, first love and best friend. He did not need to hear her story he was part of it, present for most of her triumphs as well as her tragedies. It was through him that Jazz learned the true meaning of friendship and love, a lesson she would never forget.

There amongst the various textbooks to teach her what she needed to know about academics was the first lesson in what she needed to know about love, a single red rose in her high school locker.

# The Deadliest Storm

It was only 9:00am and Jasmine Alexander was sitting in class daydreaming; but it was not your typical teenaged or childhood daydream. No, it wasn't about some guy she liked or what new clothes she wanted to buy. It was about her, Carolyn Marie Alexander AKA the deadliest storm.

It was common for Jasmine to daydream about her mother or replay some traumatic event she put her through. Today was no different. She sat there zoned out in her own private world, while tuning out the mindless chitchat around her. She didn't care who liked whom or who did what to whom. Her mind was on bigger things; like how to repair the damage left by the latest hurricane. Where did she go this time?

Carolyn had never been accused of being the most responsible person. In fact Carolyn's name had never even been mentioned in the same sentence as responsible, unless the word "not" was directly in front of it. It was no surprise that she was not exactly mother material.

When she was growing up, Carolyn was what some old folks referred to as "fast"; translation she was boy crazy! Carolyn loved boys. She always had a lot of boyfriends (usually someone else's) and at the age of 15 she became pregnant.

Since Carolyn was not exactly discriminating when it came to who she laid down with, trying to figure out who Jasmine's father could be was like playing Jeopardy. "I'll take the guy I met at the store for $200 Alex!"

Carolyn was way too young to be a mother, way to irresponsible to even be a babysitter and was advised to have an abortion. Even still a few hours after celebrating her 16th birthday (in labor) Carolyn gave birth to Jasmine anyway. Some would consider giving up your childhood to face the consequences of your actions a really mature and responsible act.

However Carolyn never really gave up her childhood; she just gave her child to her parents or anyone who happened to be around. She continued to party, hang out and live her life as if nothing happened; and her parents continued to clean up her mess as usual.

When she was a teenager Carolyn would constantly run away from home, usually to a boyfriend's house in town. She never really had any female friends' houses to go to because she had usually destroyed those relationships by sleeping with their boyfriends.

As her age increased, her radius for how far she would run increased as well. Now she would not just take someone else's man, she would take them and leave town.

Carolyn would always come back home to her family though, usually after the man she'd left with decided to use her as a punching bag when he caught her cheating; or when she ran out of money.

It wasn't because she felt guilty that her actions hurt a lot of people. She didn't care that every time the phone rang her parents were scared it was the morgue asking them to identify her body. Those things never entered her mind or her conscience.

Carolyn periodically blew through their lives like a storm, leaving destroyed feelings and hearts in her wake. This time she blew through Jasmine's college fund her grandparents saved for her. She broke their hearts and betrayed everyone's trust...except Jasmine's. She had stopped trusting her mother a long time ago.

Now nothing Carolyn did surprised her; it just increased the boulder of hate that already weighed on her chest. "Beeeeep" the bell sounded to end 1st period and snapped Jasmine out of her trance. "Dang, I wasted a whole hour daydreaming! I hope my girl Nadia took good notes!" Jasmine thought as she gathered her things to leave.

"Hey Jazz you alright? You looked like you were hypnotized over there." Nadia said as they headed to lunch. Not wanting to get into what was really on her mind, Jasmine said "I'm cool; Mrs. Hawkins is just so boring it was hard to pay attention". Nadia laughed "I know right, she is like one of those stepford chicks from that movie! But are you sure you're ok though? You looked like it was something pretty serious on your mind".

Knowing that Nadia would eventually dissect her story, Jasmine needed to take a minute to clear her head. "Yeah I am good girl. Hey I will meet you in the cafeteria I have to get something out of my locker". Still looking skeptical, Nadia said "Ok but hurry up, Chase probably has some new drama to spill and you know you can't miss a minute of that". Hurrying down the hall Jasmine said "It will just take a minute".

Standing at the locker Jazz tried to shake thoughts of her mother out of her head. When she opened the locker she saw a note from her boyfriend TJ that simply said "Have I told you how much I love you lately". Jasmine smiled; and for a brief moment Carolyn was not haunting her thoughts. TJ had that effect on her.

Since the first day they decided to share a locker, TJ started the tradition of leaving notes and sometimes gifts in the locker for each other. The first note simply said "I care about you" attached to a red rose. From that day forward Jasmine and Terrence were best friends and inseparable. Closing the locker, Jasmine felt the note was enough to help her get through the rest of the day without thinking about Carolyn. She was wrong.

"Dang girl I was about to think somebody stuffed your ass in that locker you took so long!" Chandler quipped as Jasmine entered the cafeteria. "Ha Ha Ha, you are such a comedian" Jasmine retorted as she sat down. Chase was in the middle of dishing the latest dirt. "Ya'll know that fine ass Troy Atkins is going to be dunking all over those Westwood boys tomorrow at the basketball game!"

Adding her own addendum to the Troy saga Chandler stated "Yeah and his ex-girlfriend 'Carmen the psycho senorita' will be there faking like he didn't give her crazy ass the boot last week!" Everyone laughed remembering the scene Carmen made at the last game when Troy embarrassed her by breaking up with her in front of everyone.

Carmen had come up to Troy to congratulate him after winning the game against Centerville and he ignored her. She tried to hug him and he pushed her away. Then when she started screaming and throwing one of her usual volatile tirades, he told her that he could not take her crazy mood swings and constant drama anymore so he was done with her.

Carmen lost it and started hitting Troy while crying and screaming that he could not leave her. Security tried to pull her off of Troy and she started kicking and scratching them too. It was a big mess and the "psycho senorita" as she was dubbed that night, had to wait in a holding cell until her mother came to pick her up.

The girls continued to laugh and joke about that night and discuss Nadia's crush Troy. "I guess now that the psycho senorita is out of the way, you finally got a shot at Troy" Chandler said smirking at Nadia. "Forget you trick, I don't even like that boy" Nadia shot back knowing that Troy was the leading man in every day dream she has had since he moved to Jordan Springs last year.

"Oh don't even try it Nadia, you know that boy has had your nose open since he moved here." Chase chimed in. "Whatever, next subject; are you guys still staying at my house after the game?" Nadia inquired trying to avoid the current topic. The girls continued to talk about their plans for the weekend and joke about various events that happened during the past week, while Jazz's thoughts started to drift.

Sitting there laughing with her friends and talking about typical teenaged gossip Jazz almost felt like a normal teenager with a normal life, but she wasn't. And pretty soon the reminder of just how abnormal her life was crept back into her thoughts and she was once again swept into the winds of the storm that was her life.

Drifting off into her own private world, Jazz was once again consumed by thoughts of the deadliest storm she had ever survived...her mother. Where and who did she blow off to this time? Wherever and whoever it was I hope someone warned them to lock up their men and protect their hearts, because there is a storm coming and she's deadly.

# Like Peanut Butter and Jelly

Standing on the subway platform, Jasmine felt the cold wind blowing frosty kisses across her face. As she swept her long black hair behind her ear, she caught sight of two young lovers kissing and she smiled as her mind traveled to him. Miles Davis Chase…a tall caramel brown skinned brother with an athletic build and a smile that could make you feel the sun shining in the middle of a snowstorm.

Miles…the man who made her believe in dreams again, Miles…the one who knew her better than anyone, Miles…the peanut butter to her jelly. But, in order to understand their connection…their bond, you have to understand who they are as individuals, to truly understand that…you have to go back to the beginning.

# Miles

Miles Davis Chase was born September 9, 1974 to James and Loretta Chase. James Chase was a serious jazz fan and musician…in fact that was about the only thing he was serious about, so when he had a son, he gave him the name of his favorite musician...Miles Davis.

James Chase idolized Miles Davis and he always swore he would be the next great trumpet player to share his gift with the world. But James spent his entire life doing just what his name implied...chasing his dreams. He left Miles and his mother when Miles was only three years old.

Initially, he would come to see Miles every month, then every 6 months…each time filling his head and heart with fake promises of father son outings and family trips to Disney Land that never happened. Instead, with each visit all James ever left behind for his son were tears that Loretta had to wipe away; a broken promise she had to explain away; and a broken heart

that she could never quite mend for her
son.

After his last visit Loretta sat hugging
her now six year old son, trying to soothe
the latest in a long history of disappoints
by her estranged husband. She tried to
remember why she ever fell in love with
James Earl Chase in the first place. Her
mind traveled back to when they first met.

Loretta was just 18 years old at the
time, wide eyed and very naïve. With her
curvaceous body and pecan tan
complexion, she could give Pam Grier a
run for her money on any day of the week.

Loretta was still living at home and
working as a cashier in a local drug store.
She was an obedient and shy young
woman who rarely went out, besides the
occasional trip to the mall or movies with
friends…that was until her friend Jeanette
suggested that they check out a local bar
and grill called Joe's.


Loretta had borrowed a sexy black

halter top with matching black hot pants
and Go-Go boots from Jeanette's closet.
Her naturally curly hair which she usually
wore in a ponytail, was now hanging free
resting just below her shoulders and
partially covering a pair of large gold hoop
shaped earrings. Glossy red lipstick clung
to her full sensuous lips; and the Channel
No. 5 that she was wearing compliments
of the tester bottle at the perfume counter
at the mall, left a hypnotic effect on all the
men she walked past.

Her new look was so surprising that
Loretta felt like she was playing the part of
someone else's life in a movie. While still
in awe of her amazing transformation, her
leading man entered stage right (from the
back room).

"Wow, I must have died and gone to
heaven because I swear I am looking at an
angel". Loretta was about to tell the
stranger that his line had to be the corniest
thing she had ever heard, but when she
looked up into the eyes of what had to be
the most gorgeous man she had ever seen,
all she could do was smile.

"Hey sexy momma my name is James, what's yours?" Still smiling and blushing, she placed her hand in his outstretched palm and replied, "Loretta...Loretta Davis". Loving the effect he was having on her, he continued, "Well Loretta Davis, maybe you will give me a chance get to know you better". Giggling and showing her obvious inexperience with male compliments, Loretta responded "Maybe". "Why don't we go outside and talk" James offered with plans of seeing if Loretta's lips were as juicy and sweet as they appeared. "Ok" she replied and accompanied James outside.

That was the beginning of the end for Loretta. James charmed her into giving him her phone number at work (since her father would never approve of him calling the house). Pretty soon, Loretta was using every opportunity she had to be with him. He would woo her with stories of a glamorous life as a musician in New York and shopping sprees in Paris. She was so in love with him that she would do anything he asked and it was not long before James charmed Loretta into giving him her virginity as well.

When Loretta became pregnant, James told her that he was going to marry her and that she was going to have the life of her dreams. He spun tales of how he was going to be the next Miles Davis and that they were going to live the good life in a luxury apartment on Park Ave. He told Loretta that if their baby was a boy, he wanted to name him Miles Davis Chase. Loretta agreed it was a great name for their son; of course she was so in love with James by this point any name he suggested would have been a great name.

Loretta packed her bags, picked up her last check and met James at the court house. They said their vows in front of the Justice of the Peace and then boarded a bus to New York. She left a note for her parents, telling them that she was going to live the life of her dreams with the man she loved and their expected child.

After arriving in New York pregnant,

newly married and with only $50 between them, Loretta quickly saw that that dream life James had promised was not as glamorous as she thought it would be.

Loretta and James moved into a shabby apartment above the restaurant where she was a waitress and he was a dishwasher and bus boy. Money was tight and James started to feel the pressure of having a young pregnant wife and a dream of being a musician that was not coming true as quickly as he expected.

On September 9, shortly after midnight Loretta's water broke and so did James' spirit. He was suddenly faced with the reality that he was 20 years old and had a wife and child that he now had to take care of. He began to grow bitter and blamed his non-existent music career on his wife and son.

Soon, things became really tense in the house and Loretta found herself home alone a lot with her son. This continued until Miles was about three years old. Then Loretta found that her husband stopped coming home at all.

One day after returning from her shift with Miles in tow, she found a note from James saying that he needed time to get his head straight and pursue his music career. He came around for a while periodically feeding Loretta lies about potential job offers to play in a band and a better life for their family.

After about three years of sporadic visits and fanciful tales, James stopped coming around all together; leaving behind a wife with a broken heart and son with a face that was an everyday reminder of the man who broke it.

(Excerpt from forth coming book: Like Peanut Butter and Jelly)

# Ghetto Nursery Rhymes

This section contains poems that have put an adult spin on some of your childhood nursery rhymes. Each poem reminds you that this world can be a cold place and if you make the wrong choices, you will quickly find out that life is not a fairy tale!

# Mary Had a Little Vial

Mary had a little vial whose contents
looked like snow

And everywhere that Mary went the vial
was sure to go

For another hit of coke Mary would be
your hoe

If you supply what feeds her high, there's
no limit to where she'll go

# Hickory Dickory Dock

Hickory dickory dock, three hustlers are
on the block

With one drive by…one of them will die,
the other arrested by cops

Hickory dickory dock, one hustler left on
the block

But he's a sucka and dumb motherf**ka
whose punk ass just got shot

# Three Blind Hoes

Three blind hoes…trying to work the stroll

Three blind hoes…trying to play their role

They sell their body night after night

So their pimp they won't have to fight

They value this man more than their life,
those three blind hoes

# Little Black Horner

Little Black Horner stands on the corner
trying to feed his high

As it seems…his life and dreams…have
all but past him by

Was once the man with all the plans who
considered himself a Mack

Served his country in Viet Nam and was
welcomed home by Smack

He believed the lie…that a job they'd
supply so he would not be broke

But here he stands in his homeland and
finds it was all a joke

So Little Black Horner took his place on
the corner, lost his kids and wife

With junkies by his side he takes the ride
that will surely take his life

## Life Is a Game

Life like sand slips through your hands
and can quickly pass you by

No way to slow it and before you know it,
it's your time to die

The time you spend until your end is
completely up to you

But do it right, and keep your thing tight

Cause when you're through, you're
through

So heed the words that you just heard
cause one life is all you get

So if you screw up, you're just out of luck
cause this game has no reset

# The Old Woman Who Lived in a Cell

There was an old woman who lived in a cell, when asked how she got there, this story she'd tell:

The last thing I remember, I was leaving the bar... I had my usual drinks and headed to the car.

My friend said she would drive, but I said "I'm alright"...."I do this same routine almost every night."

"Besides, I drive better drunk. I never crashed before"...It's strange after that I don't remember anymore.

I woke up in the hospital with a cut on my head. They said I would recover, but the girl I hit was dead.

They said it was her prom night and she had dressed with care...But because of my choices she never made it there.

They said she was a good kid, never smoked, drank, or lied…They said she was not at fault, but because of me she died.

I don't understand what happen. I thought it would be fine…I mean people drink and drive home all the time.

I've never had a ticket, I've never gotten caught…How could this girl's death possibly be my fault?

As I wake from my drunken haze, reality sets in…Not to mention the withdrawal symptoms started to begin.

No happy hour here to get me through the day…My choices put me in jail, and here is where I'll stay.

I'm starting to feel sick now, I feel like I am dying…I start to sweat, my stomach cramps, and I now I can't stop crying.

But no one cares about my pain because of what I've done. If someone had to die that night, I should have been the one.

So I lie here shaking in a pool of my own vomit. The C.O walked by and gave me the eye, but never made a comment.

How did I get here? I don't use drugs, I just like to drink! Alcohol is harmless right? That's what I used to think.

The judge gave me 10 years, but I probably do just three. See I'm dying from what years of alcohol have done to me.

My kidneys now are useless, my liver is decayed…My heart is barely pumping and needs to be replaced.

I guess I should be sad, but death is a welcomed sight. I still see that girl's face in my dreams every night.

I think about all the choices that I chose to make. I hope that you choose differently or you may share my fate.

Well I have to leave you now. I fear my time is done. Just think about my story, while you're out having fun.

If you have a problem, seek help now and
don't wait! Because as you see tomorrow
just might be too late!

# Meet the Author

Marquita Danielle Siler AKA

嵐 Storm

Hello everyone! I just wanted to take this time to thank you for buying and reading my book. Wow, it has been a long journey getting here and I have only just begun. Before I go any further, let me formally introduce myself and tell you a few vital statistics. My name is Marquita Danielle Siler, but I perform as and write under the name of STORM. Although I was born in and currently reside in the District of Columbia, I was raised primarily by my grandparents in Siler City, North Carolina; and yes it is as small as it sounds.

I attended Clark Atlanta University in Atlanta, Georgia where I received my Bachelor of Arts degree in Psychology. After graduation, I moved back to the District and attended the George Washington University. There, I received a Graduate Certificate in Job Development and Placement and a Master of Arts degree in Education and Human Development.

Along the way, I also obtained a Certificate in Therapeutic Massage from the National Massage Therapy Institute in Falls Church, Virginia; and I developed two companies: Visions of Serenity, LLC and Dreams in Motion, LLC, which hosts monthly talent showcases.

Now that we have the boring statistics out
of the way, let me tell you a little about
WHO I AM as a person. Let's take it from
the top shall we (I'm the little cutie in pig
tails in the lower left corner  :0). That's
my mother (who most people think is my
older sister, Suzette Siler) in the lower
right hand corner; her mother (my
grandmother and best friend, Yvonne
Siler) in the top left corner; my
grandmother's father (my great
grandfather, William T. Graves "Daddy
William" to most and dearly missed by all,

138

especially me); and his father (my great-great grandfather and the patriarch of the Graves family, Alexander Graves, RIP "Grandpa Alec").

As for me, I feel that I am now in the self-actualization stage of my life. Every day I think that I learn something new about myself that I did not know or realize before. Some of its good and some of it I feel I need to work on, but all of it is a result of my life and experiences.

My family is one of the most important and influential aspects of my life, especially my mother and my grandparents. Although I feel I am very much my own person, I have discovered certain aspects of myself that have been influenced by these three individuals.

I consider myself to be a sociable, friendly, kind, sympathetic individual, who is also generous, trusting and understanding. I can also be very persuasive and a very good negotiator when it is a subject I am passionate about

(In fact, that is one of the reasons I thought that law was my niche). I definitely bring enthusiasm to a project that sparks my interest and even if things in my personal life are falling apart, I can still appear self-confident.

My outlet for my frustrations is writing. I love poetry, music, art, films, and plays. These are things that help keep me sane and are representative of the artistic side of my personality. That is why this book is so important to me. It is me exposed. My feelings, dreams, experiences, trials and triumphs are all laid out for your inspection. This book is a look into my soul.

It is no surprise that the three people that influenced my upbringing, each influenced one side of my personality. My artistic side comes from my mother, who herself is very creative and expressive in writing. I inherited my social side from my grandmother, who is always trying to help someone and always has a kind word, friendly smile, and hot plate of food for

whoever needs it. If you have ever had the
pleasure of meeting my grandfather Jazz
Siler, it is obvious who influenced my
enterprising side. My "Daddy" has always
been the self-confident, dominant,
ambitious, and persuasive person in my
life. He is my hero and my heart.

These very different individuals and my
past experiences influence the person I
was and have become, and I carry these
pieces of each of them around in my heart

as well as my soul. I came from them, and
they are me.

(Top, my mother Suzette Siler; Left, my
grandfather Jazz Siler; and Right, my
grandmother Yvonne Siler)

## Beware of the Storm...She is Vicious!

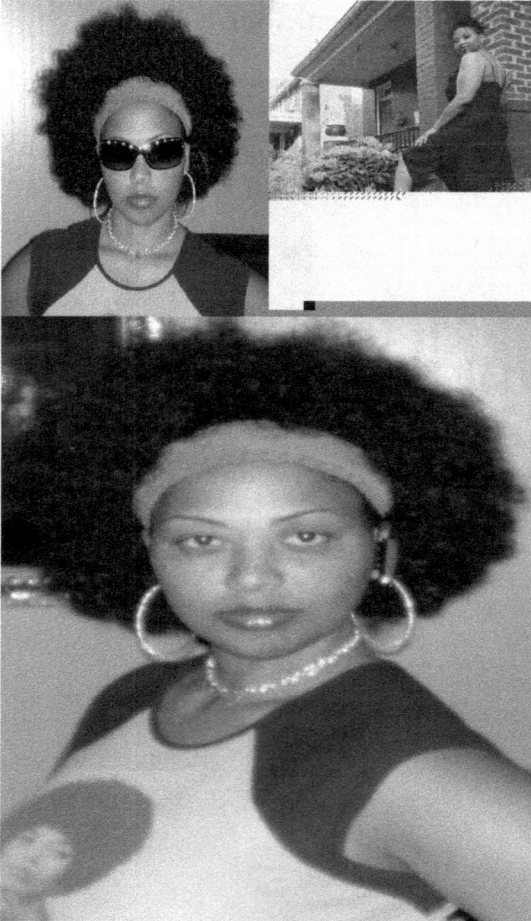

**Storm's Circle of Artist Support**

"Greetings, I would like to express that the talent and the love which are being shared on Dreamsinmotion.biz has inspired me to share my thoughts even more every day". - **EUSTACE M. BELLILLE – Author of the books *Undiscovered Thoughts*; and *Crickets in My Bed***

"Dreams in Motion make ordinary people into stars. So I thank them and wish them all the Best in the world, but they do not need my blessing so I'll leave you with this: BEWARE of the STORM. Her Dreams are already IN MOTION". - **Lamont Carey-Actor (*The Wire*) Poet (spoken word CD *Imagine*); Producer and C.E.O. of LaCarey Entertainment**

"Every Time I read your Bio, I'm inspired. Your smile is contagious. Your call name may be Storm, but you are as sweet and personal as a Queen of the Nile should be. Nourish your positive side and you will go far". - **James Bradford – Author of the book *As I Muse***

"It was inspirational to experience your poetry open mic night as well as your beautiful spirit. May GOD bless your vision and manifest it in your life". - **C.J.**

**Gross – Executive Director of ULife, Inc.**

"Storm, I am excited about what you are doing for our community. I look forward to working with you in the future". - **Nichole Patterson - Women of Excellence, Chair**

"I've heard it said that if you're holding hands with blessed people, your life must be the same. And I am so very blessed to have met you and that I am connected to your vision- it's beautiful. Keep doing what you're doing and people will not just follow, but grow. I smile with the thought that there are still people who love good and that's motivation to not just keep on loving, but also to teach others the beauty of love and who He is: Jesus. Storm, keep strong, unmovable, and encouraged- we need you." - **Tiera George – Poet & Spoken Word Artist**

"I am so proud of you Marquita aka Storm. GOD has blessed you with pure, raw talent and the brain capacity to execute anything that you set your mind to. Keep it up baby girl. GOD has more in store for you!!" - **DeShon Toussaint** –

I guess all the hype about you being this deep, introspective, poetic person is not hype after all. Keep it up Storm, and may your showers sooth us all. – **Ronnie Robinson - Poet**

"Providing a sounding-board for such discontent within an artistic context, Siler adds to her resume of youth work a strong following in entertainment and art. She coordinates monthly poetry slams where locals can share their artistry and activism in one swoop. Bonnie Duffy-Page, a grandmother who resides in Southeast and is a regular at Siler's monthly slams enjoys the release she gets when able to read her poetry "I just love it," she says. Choosing different venues to host her event, Siler boasts a loyal following that supports her efforts". - **KHADIJAH ALI-COLEMAN – excerpt from the article *"Richest Treasures East of the River"* featured in • EAST OF THE RIVER, July 2006**

"Congratulations Storm!!! You are doing it BIG! Let me know when you're doing something...I would really like to come

out and support". -**Mike Flowers – Actor**
(*Steve Harvey Show, Sister, Sister*)

"You're amazing! A woman with so much
strength of character, fire and heart! I am
inspired by your words, touched by your
request and honored to be your friend!!"
Much Love, - **Emily Turner-
Singer/Songwriter**

"…thank you for sharing your truth
through words with the rest of us."
Peace, blessings and sunshine, -**Setra-
Poet**

"With several irons in the fire, including a
spa business and a career in the nonprofit
world, Siler is a one woman tour de force.
Her Dreams in Motion events have grown
from an occasional affair to a monthly
meeting place for a faithful following who
include performers and patrons of the arts
hailing from East of the River and other
parts of the DC metro area……Without
reading from a paper and embracing the
audience with her eyes, Siler seductively
recited her poem then seamlessly segued
back into the competition and introduced
the next act." - **KHADIJAH ALI-
COLEMAN – excerpt from the article**

**"*Dreams in Motion from Southeast to Northwest*" featured in • EAST OF THE RIVER, February 2007**

# To My Friends and Family

I would like to say thank you to everyone who has supported my efforts over the years, but there are a few that I must mention by name.

**My Mother Suzette Siler**: thank you for giving me life. Although we have had our problems know that I love you as my mother. You made a choice to give birth to me; even though you were only a child yourself – thank you.

**My Grandparents Yvonne and Jazz Siler**: thank you for saving my life. No words could ever express the depths of gratitude I feel for the unconditional love and support that you have given me over the years. Although I know you may not be pleased with some of the language in this book, I know you are still proud of my accomplishment! Everything I am and will ever be, I owe to you. To say that I love you would be an understatement; to say that I owe you my life is only the beginning.

**My "Unckie" Norman:** thank you for always having my best interest at heart and always having my back. I could not have asked for a better uncle/big brother. Thanks for being there for me even if you did not know what else to do, but let me cry until my tears ran out, pass me a box of tissues and make me laugh so hard I forgot what I was crying about in the first place…I love you.

**My "Little" Cousins Patrice, Tanika & Norman Jr.** It has been an amazing gift to watch you all grow up in front of my eyes. I am so very proud of you! Know that no matter where I am or what I am doing; nothing will ever change how much I love you!

**My Cousin Rodney:** even though you are not in the same state, you are still my most supportive cousin! Thanks for always encouraging and supporting my efforts. It means more than you can ever know!

**My Cousin Laurie:** Thanks for the prayers, moral support and home cooked meals that got me through Undergrad and saved me from dorm food! I love you!

**My Cousin Bonita:** thanks for always being there for me and supporting my endeavors. Lonnell: thank you for taking such good care of my Nee-Nee. I love you both.

**My Aunt Helen and Uncle Howard:** Thanks for the love, prayers and continued support! I love you both very much!

**My Cousin Howard Jr:** June bug thanks for always letting me know how proud you are of me and showing continuous love. I love you!

**My Cousin Rickey Sr.** Thanks for being there when I need you. Debbie: Thanks for your kind and gentle spirit. I love both!

**My Cousin Rickey Jr:** Thank you for not only being my cousin, but also my friend. Leslie: Thank you for the long talks and supporting me in everything I attempt.

**My Cousin Joe:** Thank for always being there when I need you Jo-Jo. **Lisa:** you have been more than my cousin's wife; you have been my friend since the beginning. I love you both!

**My Cousin Shelley:** Thanks for making growing up in NC more interesting. When you moved away I felt like I not only lost my cousin…I lost my sister. I love you cousin!

**My Cousins Lashaunne and Monica:** Thanks for your continued support and love. I love you both!

**My DC Family:** Uncle Monroe, Ms. Janice, Aunt Burnt, Stephon, Greg, Veran, Anthony, Glen, Kevin, Tee-Tee, Monet, Michael, Mariah, Marcell, Byron, Keith, Daric, DeShannon, Nyanna, Diamond, Greg Jr., Ursel, Ursula, Chucky, Gregory, Bennie, Leslie, Keon, Baby Sis, Linda and everyone else whose name I may have missed! Thank you for the love and support!

**My New York Family:** Mary, Kenny, Travias, Case, Mia, Taleshia, Michael, Nicholas, Delores, Candace, Steven, Sylvia and everyone else whose name I may have missed. Thank you for the love, support and hospitality during my visit and always! I love you all!

**My Ohio Family:** Linda, Angie, Kevin, Kat, Deborah, Joan, Neese, Darrell, Don, Allen, Allen Jr., Candy and everyone else whose name I may have missed. Thank you for the love and continued support. I love you all!

**My NC Family:** Levi, Eddie, Rhonda, Josh, Anna, Aunt Ruth, Uncle Alfred, Alfred Jr, Vanessa, Crystal, Jarvis, Uncle Enos, Aunt Joyce, Justine, Uncle Garland, Aunt Pat, Aunt Maxine, Aunt Mary Lois, Uncle Roy, Aunt Margie, Uncle Sam, Sherry, Rhonda, Sharon, Cheryl and everyone else whose name I may have missed. Thank you for the continued love and support. I love you all!

154

**REST IN PEACE:** Alexander Graves "Grandpa Alec", William T. Graves "Daddy William", Etta Louise Graves "Mother", Lacy Siler "Grandpa Siler", Fannie Siler "Grandma Siler", Walter Graves "Sonny" Ellsworth Graves, Edward Graves, Jimmy Siler, Joyce Siler, Vivian Graves, Cathy Graves, Crystal Graves, Toni Graves, Tammy Graves and everyone else whose name I may have missed. You are truly loved and missed.

**My Pastor Rev. William Harrington** and the members of Lambert Chapel Baptist Church: Thank you for all your love, support and prayers; and for being the foundation on which I stand.

**My Little Sister Kimmy:** I am so proud of the beautiful young woman you have become and I am happy that we have reconnected. I love you baby girl! I am always here for you when you need me.

**My Homie Tosha:** thanks for being my ace, you are one of the oldest and dearest friends I have and I will always appreciate your friendship. Thanks for always being there.

**My Homie Jamie:** my other oldest friend, you will always be close to my heart. I wish you well baby boy! May you have all the love and happiness your heart can hold.

**To my Clark Atlanta University Homies, I love you all:**

**My Twin Steele:** thanks for being my brother and always being there for me through all my adventures…both good and bad. You have been my other half for so long that it is hard to remember how I got through without you. I love you, even though I am still grandma's favorite... (smile).

**My Co-Conspirator #1 and 1014 roomy for life! Cherrise aka "Ree-Ree":** I could not have picked a better roommate and friend to share my college experience with than you. I will forever be here when you need me!

**My Co-Conspirator #2Dreanna: aka "Dreanna-Weena":** What can I say…you definitely made the college experience a memorable one! In most of the antics I engaged in at college you were right there. Thanks for being my friend and a wonderful mother to two of my beautiful godchildren Dailana and Kenneth Jr.

**My Co-Conspirator #3 Treshawn: aka "Tre":** We have definitely had our ups and downs, but you were always there when I needed you; and I am glad to have you as a friend.

**My Co-Conspirator #4 Roxanne: aka "Rox":** You kept me laughing all through school with stories. With all the stunts we pulled its good that at least one of us out of the group became a lawyer…I will be sure to send you a retainer for all my future stunts!

**To my George Washington University family thanks for the love:**

**My GWU/CAU Mentor Dr. Turner:** thank you for giving me the mirror in which I saw my true self. You made me believe that my destiny was greater than the obstacles I faced. I am forever grateful.

**My Loyal Friend James:** Thanks for being a good friend and keeping me laughing! **His Wonderful Wife Liz:** Thanks for making my boy happy and keeping him in line. Although I may not make it to your events, know that I am with you both in spirit (and I promise to make at least one of your events in body as well…smile).

**To my Argosy Clique AKA "The Nation" thanks for the support:**

**My Anchor Dr. Johnson:** thanks for being the rock that kept me grounded through the storm. You have been more than a professor, you have been a teacher. You have taught me to trust myself and embrace my destiny. Thank you!

**My She-Ro Kendel:** you are the strongest person I know. Although I may not talk to you often, I talk about you all the time. You are my point of reference that we can have any life that we choose. You taught me that sometimes the road to our goals may take longer than expected, but we should make the most of the journey.

**My Road Dawg Bridgett AKA "NEAMO":** on the road to my goal, you have been the one who has shared my journey. Anytime I felt like I was in this alone, I would look over to see that you right there running beside me. Thanks for EVERYTHING and I will see you at the finish line!

**My Fellow Poet Ronnie:** thanks for making class more interesting! Now that you are married, I know that there will forever be someone there to keep you in line! Remember to always be kind to her, you are no picnic! (Smile) CONGRATS ON BEING A NEW DADDY!

**To my Dreams in Motion, Visions of Serenity and Bliss Productions Family:**

**My Event Staff Member and Loyal Supporter Keisha:** what can I say about the beautiful young woman that I watched grow up right before my eyes? I am so proud of you and all of your accomplishments! You were there before the Visions or Dreams were fully formed and you have continued to hang in there. I appreciate you more than you know.

**My Event Coordinator and Co-Defendant Kendra AKA Vixen:** you were there when all my Visions were just Dreams. Thanks for being my Cheerleader when I needed encouragement, my support when I felt like giving up and my friend always!

**My Partner and My Twin Spirit Rob AKA Bliss:** It is rare to meet someone who can not only share your vision, but expand on it as well. You are definitely a rare find. Thanks for supporting my vision, sharing yours with me, being protective (smile) and making me laugh so hard my face turns red (you know we dark children have to stick together (wink). You make work fun and my life easier. Thanks for having my back.

**My DCCIL Family** I appreciate your continued support in my endeavors and I love you all!

**My Teacher, Mr. Simms:** I would be remiss in not mentioning the impact you have had on both my career and my life. I have learned a great deal under your tutelage. You have afforded me the opportunity to amass a substantial resume of experience in both my profession and life in general. As with any form of relationship you develop with people you will have ups and downs, but regardless of the "glitches" I hope you know that I am forever grateful for the opportunities, support and encouragement you have given me! May God Bless You and May Heaven Smile Down Upon You and Your Family!

**Last But Certainly Not Least, To My Covenant House Washington Family:**

**My Champion Milton Hopkins:** you gave me the resources to reach my goals and the encouragement to not let the negativity of others make me forget the positive blessings God placed in my life. I will forever be grateful to you!

**My Surrogate Father David Young:** I know that you are smiling down from heaven. I pray that you knew how much I appreciated the support and encouragement you gave me to reach my goals; and for standing up for me when others tried to block them. Rest in Peace David and know that you are truly missed.

**My Surrogate Mother, Role Model and Friend Valarie Ashley:** for someone who has built a career on her ability to use words, I am at a loss for them. I do not believe that Webster created a word that could fully relay the impact you have made on my life. You always encouraged me to follow my dreams and gave me the platform on which those dreams were launched. This road I have traveled has been a rocky one and I have definitely had my share of stumbles and falls. But with each scrape, bump and bruise you were there to dry my tears, nurse my wounds and pull me back up again. I appreciate you more than you will ever know.

**My Surrogate Grandmother, Supporter and Timeless Diva E. Louise White:** thank you for showing me that the obstacles life places in our paths are merely stepping stones to our future. Your wisdom, beautiful spirit and classy demeanor served as a point of reference for more than just the youth that attended Covenant House, but for everyone else as well. Thank you!

**My Motivation, Mr. Gray:** you are a perfect example of a true leader. You have mastered the art of mixing intelligence; finesse and savoir-faire to not only achieve greatness, but to encourage others to discover the greatness in them.

**My CHW Homies, Co-Conspirators and Other People I will Never Forget:** Kana Perry-Summers, Antoinette, Dejuan Hogan, Ms. Grier, Saundra Duhart, Shavis Brown Jr., Shavis Brown Sr., Latif Rasheed, Michelle Neal, Chico Nelson, Sherrie Williams, Chris Calmease, Marcie, Derrick Wilson, Derrick Colbert, Donna Brown, Keisha, Kim Bookard, Vernell Payton, Byra Cole, John Summers, Darrin,

Pastor Joe Williams, Stacey Gray-Tucker, Sister Rosetta Brown, Ms. Margie and Ms. Judith Dobbins. Each of you has touched my life in some way and I love and appreciate you all.

**My Fellow Artists Thank You for the Support and Love Shown:** Kirk "Madd Game" Bias, Burchette "ISO" Greer and everyone at Incognito; Bonnie "Grandma" Duffy Page; Tiera George, Brian Cochran; Bliss, Sniper, E-Tazz AKA E-Diesel and Everyone at Bliss Productions; Tarik Lott, KJ, Cynthia, Gia and everyone at Soundbridge; Green Tea; Simba; Frank McComb; Jeneba Suma; Miles Folley; Tommy Chewning; Lamont Carey and Everyone at Lacary Entertainment; Joseph Briggs AKA One Wise African; Rebecca Dupass; E-Baby;

**TO EVERYONE ELSE: IF I DID NOT MENTION YOU BY NAME IT DOES NOT MEAN THAT YOU HAVE NOT HAD AN IMPACT ON MY LIFE. TO ALL MY FANS THANKS FOR YOUR LOVE AND CONTINUED SUPPORT!!!!!!! WITHOUT YOU**

**NONE OF THIS WOULD BE POSSIBLE. I LOVE YOU ALL!!!!!**

**Don't forget to log onto the website and leave a message in the guestbook and tell me what you think about the book!!!!!!!! And keep checking for show dates and book signing dates as well.**

www.ingramcontent.com/pod-product-compliance
Lightning Source LLC
Chambersburg PA
CBHW070205060426
42445CB00033B/1552